OCT 21 2008

Tsunamis

by Lisa Bullard

PULL AHEAD BOOKS
Forces of Nature

Lerner Publications Company • Minneapolis

For my cousin Eric, with love

Photo Acknowledgments

The images in this book are used with the permission of: AP Photo/APTN, pp. 4, 13, 19; © P. I. Productions/
SuperStock, p. 6; © NASA/Science Source/Photo Researchers, Inc., p. 7; © Gary Hincks/Photo Researchers,
Inc., pp. 8, 11, 12; © age fotostock/SuperStock, p. 10; © Chris Butler/Photo Researchers, Inc., p. 14; © Kimina
Lyall, p. 15; © John Russell/AFP/Getty Images, p. 16; © ullstein-Mehrl/Peter Arnold, Inc., p. 18; © Jeremy
Horner/CORBIS, p. 20; © Kees Metselaar/Alamy, p. 21; © Reuters/CORBIS, p. 22; AP Photo/CP, Deddeda
Stemler, p. 23; © Eriko Sugita/Reuters/CORBIS, p. 24; AP Photo/Apichart Weerawong, p. 26; © PCL/Alamy,
p. 27; U.S. Geological Survey/photo by Miller, D.J., p. 28.

Front cover: © Warren Bolster/Photographer's Choice/Getty Images

Lerner Publications Company
A division of Lerner Publishing Group, Inc.
241 First Avenue North
Minneapolis, MN 55401 U.S.A.

Website address: www.lernerbooks.com

Words in **bold type** are explained in a glossary on page 31.

Library of Congress Cataloging-in-Publication Data

Bullard, Lisa.
      Tsunamis / by Lisa Bullard.
          p.   cm. – (Pull ahead books. Forces of nature)
      Includes index.
      ISBN: 978-0-8225-8829-0 (lib. bdg. : alk. paper)
      1. Tsunamis—Juvenile literature. I. Title.
   GC221.5.B85 2009
   551.46'37—dc22   2007030536

Manufactured in the United States of America
1 2 3 4 5 6 – BP – 14 13 12 11 10 09

Table of Contents

A tsunami hits the coast of Thailand.

What Is a Tsunami?

A huge wall of water races up the beach. What is this monster wave? It is a **tsunami**. These waves can start in any large body of water. They are most common in the Pacific Ocean. But big tsunamis do not happen very often.

Normal waves are caused by wind. They move across only the top of the water.

Tsunamis are different. More than the top of the ocean moves. The water moves from the ocean bottom to the top.

The first wave of a tsunami moves toward the island of Sri Lanka. This image was taken from outer space.

This illustration shows how an underwater earthquake pushes water in different directions.

What Causes Tsunamis?

Tsunamis happen when lots of water is moved quickly. Underwater **earthquakes** cause most tsunamis. The moving earth pushes water up. Waves flow out in all directions. Other earth movements can cause tsunamis too. **Volcanoes** and giant **landslides** sometimes start them.

Tsunamis can be hundreds of miles long. They can travel across the whole Pacific Ocean. They can move as fast as a jet airplane!

In the deep ocean, the waves seem small. The water has lots of room to move. People in boats might not even notice the waves.

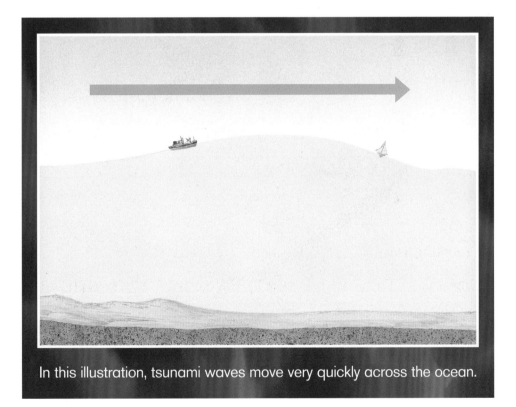

In this illustration, tsunami waves move very quickly across the ocean.

The tsunami moves toward shore. The water hits the ocean floor and slows down. It piles up on itself.

An illustration of a tsunami as it reaches shore and builds into a giant wave

Then the water rushes up the beach. Sometimes it floods the shore like a fast **tide**. Other times, it hits the shore in a giant wave.

This artwork shows how tall a tsunami can be when it hits the shore.

Some tsunamis can reach higher than 100 feet (30 meters). That's as tall as a ten-story building!

Most tsunamis are not this high. But smaller waves can still do much harm.

People run away from a tsunami in Thailand.

The Tsunami Reaches Land

The giant wave crashes onshore and moves inland. Whole towns can be destroyed. The water flattens buildings and rips up trees. It throws cars around.

Large objects in the water can hit people. Some people drown.

A tsunami destroyed these homes.

Broken trees and parts of houses cover a beach after a tsunami.

Then the water draws back into the ocean. Sometimes it sucks people into the ocean with it.

People on land are still not safe. A tsunami is a **wave train**. It has many waves. Another wave could strike.

The third wave of a tsunami crashes onto land.

Smaller waves follow a wave that pushed this boat into a city.

These waves can arrive more than an hour apart. Later waves are often bigger than the first!

The 2004 tsunami hits a hotel pool.

On December 26, 2004, a huge earthquake struck. It happened under the Indian Ocean. A giant tsunami formed.

The tsunami hit twelve countries. Over 200,000 people were killed.

Rescuers search a hotel after the 2004 tsunami.

Scientists use computers to watch for earthquakes that could cause tsunamis.

Tsunami Warnings

People did not know the giant tsunami of 2004 was coming. They did not have time to escape. Many governments are building tsunami **warning systems**. But the warnings can't always get to people fast enough.

Some countries have built **tsunami walls**.

But no wall can stop the biggest
tsunamis. They remain a danger to
people who live near oceans.

More about Tsunamis

The highest recorded tsunami was in Lituya Bay, Alaska, in 1958. A wave reached the height of over 1,700 feet (520 meters)!

Giant waves hit Lituya Bay in 1853, 1936, and 1958.

TSUNAMI FACTS

• *Tsunami* is a Japanese word. It means "harbor wave." It is pronounced soo-NAH-mee.

• Islands are at great risk from tsunamis. Tsunami waves can wrap around an island. They can hit it from all sides.

• Meteorites could cause tsunamis. A meteorite could hit the ocean. If it were big, it would move lots of water. This could start the monster waves.

• Some scientists believe that animals can sense a coming tsunami. Some animals can hear and feel things that humans can't. They may get an early warning that people don't.

• Some people have talked about living through a tsunami. One said it was like "being in a washing machine."

• In some tsunamis, ocean water is first sucked away from the beach. Flopping fish are left behind. This is a warning sign to run to higher ground! A tsunami is coming.

Further Reading

Books

Hatkoff, Isabella, Craig Hatkoff, and Paula Kahumbu. *Owen & Mzee: The True Story of a Remarkable Friendship.* New York: Scholastic, 2006.

Riley, Joelle. *Earthquakes.* Minneapolis: Lerner Publications Company, 2008.

Websites

FEMA for Kids: Tsunami
http://www.fema.gov/kids/tsunami.htm
The Federal Emergency Management Agency hosts this "FEMA for Kids" site. It has activities and information about how to stay safe if a tsunami comes to your area.

National Geographic Kids: Tsunami
http://nationalgeographic.com/ngkids/9610/kwave
This website has great drawings and information about tsunamis. It also has one girl's tsunami story.

Pacific Tsunami Museum
http://www.tsunami.org/students.html
Visit this website for tsunami information, games, and links to other great sites.

Glossary

earthquakes: shakings of Earth's surface

landslides: downward, rushing movements of dirt and rock. Landslides often run down steep hills or mountainsides.

tide: the normal rise and fall of the ocean

tsunami: a series of waves started by earth movement, such as an earthquake, a volcano, or a landslide

tsunami walls: walls built to hold back the water from a tsunami

volcanoes: openings in the ground out of which steam, bits of rock, or melted rock come

warning systems: a way to tell people that danger is coming

wave train: a series of waves one after the other

Index